Prayer

Book

Prayer Book

To Encourage Your Prayer Life

Stacey Ann Satchell

Copy Rights

My Thoughts

I don't believe prayer needs to be complicated to get to God. For me I keep it simple for I will be talking to Him throughout the rest of the day. A typical beginning of my day is just simply saying, "Thank You Lord for waking me up this morning. Reason being, the gift of life is the beginning of a new. My motto is, with life comes possibility. It's a gift and in my world its one to be highly appreciated. This very thing I say with my daughter religiously every morning, for I need her to understand the value of life. This is our typical daily routine until we get in the car. Know this scripture is true for she never makes me forget to pray before we drive off in the mornings.

Proverbs 22:6 Train up a child in the way he should go: he will not depart from it. (KJV)

Our morning prayer is pretty much always the same.

Gracious Father, we come before you presence with praise, for it is You that has given us life. Lord we ask for your covering grace as we travel throughout this day, Father we welcome the Holy Spirit to abide within us. Give us a spirit of conviction, this way all we do today will edify The Kingdom. Lord we give You all the honor and glory. Amen

This is my version of short and spicy, putting in the necessary request for all we will need for that particular day. It's a lifestyle not a quick fix so I pray for each day for God needs no help to bless us. As my day progress I make it a necessity to check in with The Lord, this way I wont stray or if I waiver some it wont be for long nor will I stray too far. My typical night is just giving thanks for all I have experience throughout 'the' day. Not forgetting to ask for forgiveness for sins known and unknown. My experiences have thought me to be extremely thankful for all things and I am sharing this prayer book in hopes of making it visible that in order to achieve we need the Lord. We are all champions for He has made us overcomers.

Table of Contents

Inspiration

Being just a babe to the Word of God, I knew not what to do; so I turned to prayer. This I practice daily, for I had lost my way after being saved for three years. From my experience I was able to grow spiritually through prayers, which lead me to the Word of God.

If you abide in Me, and my Words abide in you, you will ask what you desire, and it shall be done for you. John 15:21

However, this kind does not go out except by prayer and fasting. Matthew 17:21

Today I am successful and happy for the Lord is head of my life. So I encourage you to turn to the one who is able to do exceedingly above all our imagination. He done it for me, and so will He for you.

And whatever things you ask in prayer, believing, you will receive. Matthew 21:22

I also practice to insert scriptures in my prayers, this way His word is within me.

(Scriptures Are Highlighted)

Awe

Behold, thus shall the man be bless who fear the Lord.

So I worship You Lord in holy attire.
I come in Your presence, with grace and meekness.

Let Your mercy be upon me, and my family and in
everything we do.

 Lord, keep me in fear of Your name.

I ask of You to keep me mindful of Your will.

Turn me from everything that is not of You.

Make my heart tremble at Your voice.

Cause me to stand up right no matter what I may loose,
and keep me encourage with your promise.

                                                        Amen

Psalm 128:4

19

Anointing

Lord, let Your anointing fall upon me.

Let Your power come into me.

Father, let Your anointing stream through my ear so I will know Your voice.

Flow through my mind and soul aligning them to follow Your Word.

Anoint my feet, so my path may be clear and your direction mine.

Now, being filled with the fruits of righteousness, which are by Jesus Christ, of the glory and praise of God.

I receive your anointing and teaching, so my way is straight at all times.

Amen

Philippians 1:11

Battle

For You have armed me with strength, for the battle; You have subdued under me those who rose up against me.

I die so you may increase in me.

Lord I put my trust in You,

For You are The Lord Our Banner.

You have concur the world for me and die so I may live.

So I live in the rewards of Your works and I offer thanksgiving, for You have equipped me with the tool to overcome.

The battle wasn't mind to begin with so I give them to You who is able.

Jehovah Nissi thanks for dwelling in me.

I receive Your presence and glorify You.

So now I walk boldly, knowing You are in me.

Amen

Psalm 18: 39

Council

You guide me by your wise advise, and then You will lead me to a position of honor.

Which I humbly receive this day.

Lord let Your will be done in me.

Elevate me Lord in every area of my life.

Let Your desires for me come alive.

So I may be that light in a dark place.

I live for You Lord, and Your will be done in me this day and forevermore.

Amen

Psalm 73:24

25

Courage

Lord inscribe in me, a spirit of no fear, so I won't be defeated.

That I be strong and of good courage, fear not, nor be afraid of them: for the LORD thy God, it is

You doth go with thee, and You will not fail thee, nor will You forsake thee.

Keep me mindful that I am of You and encourage in me to walk upright and with confidence for I have inherited Your protection.

Guide my step in the right path that I may be consistent and remain out of the demonic forces that may come up against me daily.

I surrender myself onto You Lord.

Amen

Deuteronomy 31:6

Daily

Prayer

Lord I first want to thank You for considering me yet again.

I confess my sins, those known and unknown.

Lord, give me a renewed mind that I may confront the challenges of today.

Create in me Oh Lord an overcoming Spirit that I may triumph over the trials set before me.

Giving me serenity in the things I have no control over.

Set me in the right path that I may be a blessing to others.

Dwell within me Lord, directing my step and thought.

Give me peace, understanding and patience.

Lord watch over me as I go about my way today.

Let my supplication come before thee, deliver me according to thy will.

Lord I offer up thanksgiving for all you have done and will do for me.

Amen

Deliverance

Thank You Lord for Your never-ending love for me.

Lord, You have carried me through it all.

You have allowed me to be more than a conqueror, and I thank You.

Father, I thank You for delivering me from self.

From all the situations I had put myself in.

I am eternally grateful that You have thought of me before this day.

Sending, **Your only begotten Son to die for my sin, so I may have life more abundantly.**

For though I was born in sin, I don't have to remain there, for I have a choice and I choose You this day Lord.

Amen

John 3:16   (Partial Scripture Reworded)

Direction

Heavenly Father, my desires are of You, so be present in all I do.

Direct my steps by Your word; don't let any sin dominate me.

Lead me on the right path; guide me through Your wisdom.

Make my path straight despite the desires of the enemy.

Let not fear nor any evil of the world direct my path away from You.

Lead me to Your grace, mercy, and favor through faith.

Amen

Psalm 119:133

33

Faith

Heavenly Father, grant me understanding.

Encourage in me a spirit of patience that I may wait upon You.

Take from me all negative character, which will hinder me from Your will.

Lord I seek a discerning spirit of Your word.

So birth in me unlimited faith; keep me in remembrance of all you have done for me.

Transform my faith in You Lord, with an assurance that it is done.

Amen

Finance

You have granted me life and favor, and Your care has preserved my spirit.

Jehovah Jireh, You are the Lord that has been providing for me.

I pray for Your guidance and creative ideas that are within Your will.

Give me spiritual wisdom and understanding of money.

This way I will use the finances given me wisely.

Lord, make me a blessing to Your kingdom and others.

I am grateful Lord and giving thanks to God the Father in the name of our Lord Jesus Christ.

I pray your continual blessing over every situation to come in my life.

I sow this day thanksgiving, appreciation, and gratitude unto You Lord.

For You are my witness Lord, I long for all of You with the affection of Christ Jesus.

Amen

Philippians 1:8

Forgiveness

Forgive me Lord for I have sin.

Direct me into Your perfect will Lord.

I surrender to You my carnal self.

I ask of You to enter in.

Holy Spirit, guide me to become more Christ like.

And as I, forgive my debtors so will You forgive my debt.

Lord, cause me to become more spirit sensitive so I will recognize Your voice and understand Your directions.

I thank You Lord for an understanding spirit in the name of Jesus Christ I receive it.

Amen

Matthew 6:12

Gift

Lord I know through my faith I will receive gifts for Your mercy is never ending.

So give me sight that I may recognize my gifts and great wisdom and knowledge that I may be wise and useful with my gifts.

Whether gift of healing, help, government, diversities of tongues.

I thank You for the Spirit of the Holy Ghost, which dwell in me and teach me.

Induce in me growth, and understanding that I may excel to the edifying of the church.

Amen

1 Corinthians 12:28

41

Grace

Thank You Lord for considering me.

For all I could never accomplish You have made possible.

Without You I am nothing, but with You Lord, I am more than the whole world against me.

You are the Lord of a breakthrough.

I take this opportunity to thank You for showing up and out on my behalf.

I thank You for Your unmerited and abundant gift of love and Your unbounded favor.

For I know its nothing I have done but according to Your mercy, I am saved.

Amen

Guidance

Lord I come to You in Jesus name, thanking You for always being available to me.

As I go about my way Lord, I ask for Your guidance and direction in all my endeavors.

Guide my every step and command my way to be in line with Your Will.

I thank You Lord for going before me, and your never-ending favor in all I do,

For, **when there is no guidance a nation falls, but there is success in the abundance of counselors**.

Therefore I surrender unto You, when you move I move for my eyes are now entwine with Yours.

Amen

Proverbs 11:14

45

Healing

Jehovah Rophe the Lord who heals, I ask for spiritual, emotional as well as physical healing.

This way my thoughts and soul be in line with Your will and my physical being so I am able to help myself.

Lord renew my mind so I can know You have healed me, for Your Word declare I am made whole through my faith.

Lord build up my spirit, complete restoration I ask of You.

For when the spirit is out of line with You Lord, their lack my faith in Your power to heal me completely.

Holy Spirit, travel through my veins and bone and make me whole again.

Heavenly Father allow me to transform to Your way of living more with each day so I wont ask no more for I will know it is done.

I praise You Lord for complete restoration of my mind, spirit and physical wellbeing.

Amen

Holy Spirit

Holy Spirit I come as I am, asking you to dwell within me.

Holy Spirit I decrease so You may increase.

I give all authority to You Lord, for I have tried and fail.

I realize without You I have nothing.

I die today to the divine source of all life, so I will receive power through Jesus Christ.

I fellowship with You; Holy Spirit.

My will, thoughts, feelings are Yours, into Your hands I commit my Spirit.

Amen

49

Humility

For the fear of the LORD is the instruction of wisdom; and before honour is humility.

Lord I ask You to live within me, equipping me to fear thy name.

Transform my mind Lord align my thoughts to Your will.

Clothe me in humility Lord that I may hear Your voice and be humble throughout all my successes.

Renew in me daily a meek spirit in the highly esteem name of Jesus Christ.

Amen

Psalms 15:33

Joy

Scripture says ask **and you will receive that your joy may be fill**.

So I am here Lord asking to trade my sorrow for the joy of The Lord.

I surrender unto You Lord for I know, **you will show me the path of life, in Your presence is fullness of joy; at Your right hand are pleasure for evermore**.

So I humbly ask and receive You Lord, for in You I find life.

Gracious Father guide my every step and thoughts for I seek immeasurable joy, the kind that only You can give.

The joy of The Lord is mine, I receive You Lord and I am thankful that You know me by name and have forgiven me like only You can.

Amen

John 16:24 (Partial)

Psalm 16:11

Knowledge

Lord, align my heart with Your instructions and my ears to The Word of knowledge.

For I know to speak without knowledge is to speak words without understanding.

So Lord let Your word be clear to me, so without effort I will know what it is You desire of me for Your voice is known.

Let me be condemned by my thoughts that are not of You and increase through Your knowledge more with each day.

Give no gift nor blessings which You have not prepare for me no matter how much I ask.

Lord give me the knowledge of patience this way I wont be eager for that which You haven't provided nor prepare for me.

Give me a translucent understanding of all You place before me this way I will use them wisely and not out of lack of understanding.

Limitless knowledge I seek with a combination of humility so I wont loose my way.

Amen

Proverbs 23:12

Liberty

Beloved Father I can't fulfill Your law through my human ability.

So I ask You to manifest Your Holy Spirit in me.

Inhabit Your character in me, You exemplary love and charitable spirit.

Give me a heart to love others like you love me, and the longsuffering spirit of Jesus Christ.

Reward me with the gift of Your standards.

Holy Spirit, train my heart on Christ and conform me to love as Jesus did life and peace.

For to be carnally minded is death; but to be spiritually minded is life and peace.

I choose You Lord.

Amen

Roman 8:6

Love

For the law of the Spirit of life in Christ Jesus has made me free from the law of sin and death.

Lord, teach me to love myself. Your commandment states that I should love thy neighbor as I love myself.

So Lord I ask for Your forgiveness, for I failed in loving self.

I ask for You to birth within me the love You have shown us by sacrificing Your only begotten son Jesus Christ.

I desire Lord to be more like You. For if I can love myself the way You love me then I can fulfill Your commandment.

Love does no harm to a neighbor therefore love is the fulfillment of the law.

Lord let this Word be engrave in my heart this way I will forever treat others and myself the way You have treat us.

Amen

Romans 8:2

Romans 13:10

Mercy

Lord I know without Your unwavering
forgiveness and kindness;I would be lost.

**God be merciful to me and bless me and cause Your face
to shine upon me**.

God be merciful to me a sinner. I surrender unto
You Lord who is able to forgive all my sins.

Lord I know not what I would do without Your
mercy, for without it I would not have the gift of
eternal life.

Thank You Lord for being so gracious.

Amen

Psalms 67:1 (Reworded To Make It Personal)

Might

There is no one like You, Lord You are great. You are renown for Your power.

You have made me in your image so I have the potential hidden in me to do marvelous works.

Lord, awaken in me that mighty spirit You have created within me.

Sovereign Lord, call out all spirit that hinder me from walking boldly.

For You have given me a spirit of might and not of fear.

Open my mind this way I will understand, having all confidence that I can and I will.

I am Your child and You know me even before I was, so manifest in me Your strength Lord, and don't let me loose sight but know it is You who have bless me favorably.

I know I am nothing without You Lord.

Amen

Obedience

As newborn babes, desire the sincere milk of the word, that ye may grow thereby:

I seek Your guidance Lord, for I desire nothing more than to be obedient to Your Will.

For, then I will no longer be an infant, tossed back and forth by the waves, and blown here and there by every wind of teaching and by the cunning and craftiness of people in their deceitful scheming. Instead, speaking the truth in love, I will grow to become in every respect the mature body of him who is the head, that is, Christ.

Lord I aim to master the principle and law of You, for if I can be submissive and respectful of the Word, so will I to everything else.

So I pray this day for You to encourage in me the desire of obedience to Your Will, causing the manifestation of Your works in me.

Amen

1 Peter 2:2

Ephesians 4:14-15 (Reworded to make personal)

Patience

Holy Spirit, come in and transform me.

I have done Your Will but I am in need of some patience.

Birth in me a Spirit of endurance and perseverance while I wait on Your promise.

Lord, open my eyes so I will be able to see and my ear in tune to Your voice so I can stay focus on You.

Let my flesh die so I wont be consume or caught up in the world.

Let not my heart be troubled but in remembrance of Your love for me.

Amen

Peace

Lord I come to You in the name of Jesus.

I ask of You to guide me, oh Lord and bestow upon my life indescribable peace.

Lord for I know not how to overcome these feelings I feel today.

I turn to You Lord who is able.

Jehovah Shalom I pray for You to minister to my spirit.

I ask of You to make me whole, complete, fulfilled and perfected.

Engrave in me the kind of peace that only You can.

Create in me a whole person in right relationship of Your Word.

I thank You Jehovah Shalom for You are within me, You have renew and equip me in this season.

In the mighty name of Jesus I am complete and fulfilled.

Amen

71

Perfect Will

Lord may Your Will be done in my life.

I come to You just as I am, seeking Your guidance for my life.

I am lost without You, so I surrender my mind, body and soul to You.

I have made it up in my mind to not be lead by my natural sight but to be lead by Your Holy Spirit.

For only You can, make me perfect in every good work to do Your will, working in me that which is well pleasing in his sight, through Jesus Christ to whom be glory for ever and ever.

Amen

Hebrew 13:21

Promise

Our Father in heaven, hollow be thy name, thy kingdom come. Thy will be done on earth as it is in heaven.

This is Your written promise that I can ask for anything in Your Will and You will release it from the heavens into the earth.

Lord I come to you today seeking direction, I ask of you to come and equip me.

I seek Your promise for my life. I am dismay without You, Lord.

Truth is I know I can't get it together on my own, so I give it all to You.

Lord, I have made it up in my mind not to be directed by my natural sight but to be lead by the Holy Spirit.

I receive Your Will for my life in Jesus precious name.

Amen

Luke 11:2

75

Praise

To God

Father I come not to ask for anything but to give praises for all things.

Lord I thank You for waking me up, it's the first gift of each day and I appreciate You Lord.

Thank You for all I am able to do, for all I do is because of Your grace.

I am thankful for even the bad for it has not killed me, but has made me stronger.

Even when I not understand or see the whole picture You have kept me.

Thank You for protecting me from the unseen.

Thank You for loving me Lord, I take not for granted all You have done for me.

I appreciate You Lord and I take this time just to say Thank You.

Amen

Prayerlessness

Lord I have tried the world way and it benefit me nothing.

So I give up Lord, I put it in Your hands this day.

My soul melts from heaviness, strengthen me according to Your words.

So I may increase in You daily through prayer and supplication.

Restore in me the strength of You Lord, so I may persevere and grow increasingly in knowledge and wisdom.

Give me the zeal for Your works through prayer as I seek You.

Amen

Renewing Of The Mind

Lord I present myself as a living sacrifice, holy acceptable to You.

I ask You to change my mindset and desires.

Lord, align my thoughts with Your Word.

I cast my care unto You Lord for I know You care for me.

I release the thought of self and take on the thoughts You have towards me, thoughts of good and not of evil.

Lord let everyday be a new day for me, this way I won't carry negative thoughts into the day You have gifted me.

I pray for the gift of forgiveness this way I can release that which wasn't of You and take unto me those things that are of You.

I dedicate myself to You Lord, I seek You this day and forever more.

Amen

Romans 12:1

Righteousness

Jehovah Tsidken You're The Lord Our
Righteousness.

Direct me in the path of righteousness for the
eyes of The Lord are on the righteous, and Your
ears are open to their cry.

I have in me a hunger for You and a desire and
passion to know more of You.

For Your work is majestic and glorious and Your
faithfulness endures forever.

Lord I yield unto **You so I may be filled for, You are
just, O Lord and Your judgment are fair.**

Amen

Psalms 119:137

Sacrifices

God for You are faithful and just to forgive, and to cleanse me from all unrighteousness.

I come confessing all my sins. I decrease so You may increase in me.

You have died so I may have life more abundantly.

So I ask for you to cleanse and restore me.

Wash me with Your blood Jesus.

Keep me Lord in all I do from this day forward and forever.

Amen

1 John 1:9

Sanctification

In God

I offer thanks and loudly proclaim all You have done for me.

Jehovah M'Kaddesh, the Lord who sacrifices, consider me.

Lord it is You who have made me whole set apart for holiness.

It's by Your grace and mercy that I am consecrated and made holy.

Help me Oh Lord to keep Your decrees and follow them.

Keep me in remembrance that You are the Lord who sanctify.

I give myself to You Lord, so I can be use for the up building of Your Kingdom.

Lord I know the liberating truth that my needs can only be found in You.

Dwell here Heavenly Father wash me with Your loving kindness, vindicate me Lord.

Amen

Sinners Prayer

Father, You have been faithful and just to forgive me.

I recognize my unfaithfulness to You so I surrender unto You.

Sins that I have committed, those known and unknown I place before You.

Forgive me precious Lord for I knew not what I have done.

I receive You Lord. Save me from myself precious Lord, heal my wicked ways.

Make me whole. Deliver me by renew in me a righteous character.

Wash away all my iniquity. Cleanse me of sins. Free me from myself.

Conform me to the purpose set aside for me, in Jesus name.

Amen

Spiritual

Growth

Lord for You have known me before I was
formed in the womb and set me apart.

Today I come before You seeking complete
restoration in knowledge, wisdom,
understanding, inspiration for Your will,
compassion, gratitude and happiness.

Redeem in me a hunger and thirst for You. Give
me confidence that way I know I have the
petition to do Your will for You created me in
Your own image.

Keep me in remembrance of Your power which
is within me.

Bring growth to my spiritual life that I may walk
upright and take my position in the body of
Christ for the Kingdom.

Humble me as I grow this way I will stay
committed to Your Will for my life.

                                                    Amen

Spiritual

Power

For the Lord as declared, that whosoever shall say unto this mountain, Be thou removed, and be thou cast into the sea; and shall not doubt in his heart, but shall believe that those things which he saith shall come to pass, he shall have whatsoever he saith.

So with the power the Lord has manifested in me, I say to my physical ability you are whole.

Broken relationship, I have overcome You. Career, business venture, whatever I believe in is mine in the mighty name of Jesus.

I reclaim my spiritual power of healing I cast out all negativity that shall come against me.

To my mind, those thought aren't mine; I declare it gone! My soul is restored and my heart is for the Lord.

All power, thee given me, I declare no arm, no evil or demonic presence can come against me.

Victory is mine for I inhabit the divine power of healing and have been restored in every area. Everyone in my life shall prosper and every good thing is mine and I receive it in the name of Jesus for it is done.

Amen

Mark 11:23

Spiritual

Strength

For I know Oh Lord You are able to **renew my strength that I not become weary nor faint.**

I come to You with open arms surrendering all. Giving thanks for Your Holy Spirit.

Guide me to the way of truth; help me restore my spiritual path and practice.

Keep me an overcomer of daily trials. Dwell in my heart that I may inhabit the agape love that will surpass knowledge.

Add to my faith great patience so that I wont be mislead.

Give me a discerning spirit to deal with Your people and life.

I hand it all over to You, so strengthen me with might by Your Spirit.

Amen

Isaiah 40:31 (Partial)

95

Strength

Lord I know with strength comes trial, so I pray this day to be equipped for the trials and tribulations to come.

Lord I ask You to keep me in remembrance that for everything I overcome its for the edification of Your Kingdom.

Thank You Lord for the strength You have given me to triumph over all my trials which will one day be my testimony which will be a blessing unto someone.

Thanks for giving me understand for those things I never overcome in an instant for You where there along the way and I am grateful You never gave up on me.

I am honored You chose me Lord, even though it wasn't easy I am well please that I could be used.

Thanks be to God, who always leads me in triumphal procession in Christ and through me spreads everywhere the fragrance of the knowledge of him.

Amen

2 Corinthians 2:14

Thanksgiving

I enter into Your gates with thanksgiving, For You have been good to me and Your mercy is everlasting.

I thank You Lord for first another bless fill day, another opportunity to make it right.

Another day to be a blessing, thank You Lord for allowing me to continue Your perfect Will for my life.

I thank You for Your grace and limitless favor on my life.

I am grateful for You have qualify me to be partaken of Your inheritance.

It is a gift Lord and I receive it and I am mindful of this blessing.

Lord, thank You for loving me, even when I don't love myself.

I make the choice to serve You and I am grateful to You for receiving me as Your child.

I give thanks in everything for it's the will of God through Jesus Christ.

Amen

Psalms 100:4-5

Understanding

Give me understanding so that I might observe Your law, and keep it with all my heart.

Give me insight through wisdom so I can live an esteem life.

Keep this knowledge apart of me so I may remain in Your grace and be worthy to deserve abundant life.

Help me to use this knowledge in my daily life.

Lord, give me revelation in all I do and hear.

For, the wisdom that comes from heaven is first of all pure; then peace-loving, considerate, submissive, full of mercy and good fruit, impartial and sincere.

So fill me up Lord.

Amen

James 3:17

Wisdom

By wisdom a house is built, and through understanding it is establish.

So I come to You humble, seeking your wisdom for my life.

Lord, instill in me the knowledge of You.

Let my heart be receptive to Your Word and voice.

I ask for the guidance of the Holy Spirit.

This way I have an understanding knowledge of Your desires for my life.

Give me a sense of direction so I may walk upright knowingly.

Thank You Lord

Amen

Proverbs 24:3

Virtue

Lord Jesus, I come seeking this day a perfect bond with You, so I may stand steadfast on Your word.

Develop my knowledge that I may speak wisdom over my life and to others.

Cause me to be sensitive and thankful for all things.

For; according as Your divine power hath given unto us, all things that pertain unto life and godliness, throw the knowledge of God that hath called us to glory and virtue.

Father, make me a woman of excellence when it come to Your Will.

Amen

2 Peter 1:3

Childs

Prayer

Thank You Lord for waking me up.

Thank You for my mom and dad.

Thank You for my friends and my teachers.

Thank You for everything Jesus.

Thank You for taking care of everybody Jesus.

Thank You, Thank You, Thank You.

                                        Amen

© Shaniece Hansen

Teen

Gracious Father, I thank You for considering me.

I am grateful for this day and I am looking forward
to the rewards ahead.

Lord I ask of You to give me a clear
understanding of my teachers today.

I ask for Your guidance to and from school
today,

I thank You for my parents and the food I will
partake in this morning.

Lord I thank You for my family and Your never
ending blessings on our lives.

Amen

Adult

Lord I receive this day which You have set before me and I am full commit to making the best of it.

Father I invite You to entering in, I need You this day.

Holy Spirit I thank You for Your presence and I ask for Your direction through this day.

Being fully convinced that what You had promised Your are also able to perform.

Therefore I put before You everything, from our going out to our coming in.

Lord I ask You to guide my every step. Keep me mindful of my surrounding, activities and thoughts.

Set favor before me in every area of my life.

All honor and glory is Yours Lord and I just want to say Thank You for loving me.

Amen

Romans 4:21

Bedtime Child

As I lay down to rest, I thank You for watching over me Lord.

Tonight have Your angels to watch over me as I sleep.

Thank You for my family and I ask that You grant me another day.

Looking forward to a marvelous tomorrow Lord.

Amen

Bedtime

Teen

Heavenly Father I thank You for all you are doing in my life.

For blessing me with wonderful parents and keep blessing them Lord.

Thank You for giving me the knowledge to understanding what I learn at school today.

I pray for Your forgiveness in all I have done against Your will and ask for guidance so I make better choices.

Lord I ask for You to anoint my ear and heal my mind, this way I will ear the right things and I will not be affected by the pressures of my peers.

Lord I thank You for Your love, grace and mercy.

I am grateful for this day and pray for another.

Amen

Bedtime

Adult

Glory be to my Father which is in heaven.

I thank You Lord for once again blessing me with life.

Thank You for covering me throughout this day.

Watch over me tonight and bless me with another day.

I ask for my forgiveness, those known and unknown.

As I sleep tonight Lord birth in me creative ideas and renew
and prepare me for a brand new day.

I declare rest over my body in Jesus name.

Amen

To You

I do pray I was able to encourage your prayer life. I pray that you will begin to see the manifestation of pray. That it's the key to obtaining the power to fight all negativity that shall try to come upon you. I take this opportunity to encourage you to stay focus on the Word of God _____, for every trial or situation you will ever face _____ the answer on how to overcome is written in the Word.

Please be fruitful by touching another's life through your knowledge of God.

So shall the knowledge of wisdom be unto thy soul, when thou hast found it, then there shall be a reward, and thy expectation shall not be cut off.

Proverbs 24:12

Thank you again for your support, I sincerely appreciate you.

Make it personal by writing your name on the line above.

My Conclusion

I believe the said promise given in the days of
Abraham is also ours. It's our inheritance and it is
necessary to tap into it for the fulfillment of our lives.
Jesus made a covenant with His people but in todays
generation I believe that covenant is greater. Choose
to see Him through the Word and in prayer. I choose
to inject scriptures in my prayers for I believe this is a
way to inscribe His Word in our hearts. For me I find
myself doing it unknowingly. Sometimes I catch on
but how many times is there that I didn't even give
notice that I have. One thing for sure is this, The Lord
never not give notice to our actions. Therefore I count
it a blessing and not a loss. My last words to you are
to practice pulling for the Word always, making it
apart of your everyday life. Soon you too will be doing
it unknowingly. Whenever I read the things I write I
always have to pull for my Bible for confirmation. All
things come from The Lord but I always have to make
sure that it isn't scriptures that I have written has my
own.

Scriptures keep us mindful of the choices we make for
the closer He is to us the more accessible He will be
when we need Him. This is reason enough to dwell in
His presence always. He will convict us when
necessary, which will keep us in line with His will for
our life. He will be there to cheer us when we need it

most. Truth is we are never alone but we have to know the how to connect with The Lord. Don't let the noise of the world greater than His. His promise for our lives is revealed in His word. Make it apart of your life so you don't live to just exist but to prosper, as He desires you to.

It's my belief that the way we ask is the way we receive, this is why its so important to get in line with His will. Be in sync with The Lord for it's the only way. Scripture says out of the mouth comes life and death, blessings and curse so my thoughts are to speak life.

Stacey Ann Satchell

My Book

Contacts

Company Name: Stacey Ann Satchell

Author: Stacey Ann Satchell

My Websites:

www.staceyannsatchell.com

www.wrapmeinyourarmsinc.com

My Email:

staceyann.n.satchell@gmail.com

Social Media:

Facebook:
www.facebook.com/StaceyAnnSatchell

Instagram:
www.instagram.com/Staceyann_Satchell

Twitter: www.twitter.com/Stacey_Satchell

www.ingramcontent.com/pod-product-compliance
Lightning Source LLC
Chambersburg PA
CBHW071558040426
42452CB00008B/1219